1st Recital Series

FOR Bb BASS T.C./B.C.

Including works of:
- James Curnow
- Craig Alan
- Mike Hannickel
- Timothy Johnson
- Ann Lindsay

Solos for Beginning
through Early Intermediate
level musicians

CURNOW® MUSIC

Edition Number: CMP 0850.03

1st Recital Series
Solos for Beginning through Early Intermediate level musicians
B♭ Bass T.C./B.C.

ISBN: 90-431-1912-1

CD Accompaniment tracks performed by Becky Shaw

CD number: 19.044-3 CMP

Foreword

High quality solo/recital literature that is appropriate for performers playing at the Beginner through Early Intermediate skill levels is finally here! Each of the **1st RECITAL SERIES** books is loaded with exciting and varied solo pieces that have been masterfully composed or arranged for your instrument.

Included with the solo book is a professionally recorded CD that demonstrates each piece. Use these examples to help develop proper performance practices. There is also a recording of the accompaniment alone that can be used for performance (and rehearsal) when a live accompanist is not available. A separate Piano Accompaniment book is available [edition nr. CMP 0855.03].

Table of Contents

Track			Page

1   Tuning Note Bb Concert

Bb Bass T.C.

Track		Title	Page
2	3	A Summer Walk	5
4	5	Soliloquy For Tuba	6
6	7	Trinidad And Tobago	7
8	9	Kum Ba Yah	8
10	11	Polonaise For Polar Bears	9
12	13	Carnival	10
14	15	Faith Of Our Fathers	11
16	17	Hungarian Dance No. 6	12
18	19	Tuba Holiday	13
20	21	Tuba Dances	14
22	23	Aria	15
24	25	In The Hall Of The Mountain King	16

Bb Bass B.C.

Track		Title	Page
2	3	A Summer Walk	17
4	5	Soliloquy For Tuba	18
6	7	Trinidad And Tobago	19
8	9	Kum Ba Yah	20
10	11	Polonaise For Polar Bears	21
12	13	Carnival	22
14	15	Faith Of Our Fathers	23
16	17	Hungarian Dance No. 6	24
18	19	Tuba Holiday	25
20	21	Tuba Dances	26
22	23	Aria	27
24	25	In The Hall Of The Mountain King	28

☐   *Solo with accompaniment*

■   *Accompaniment*

1. A SUMMER WALK

Mike Hannickel (ASCAP)

Copyright © 2003 by **Curnow Music Press, Inc.**

2. SOLILOQUY for TUBA

Craig Alan (ASCAP)

Expressively (♩ = 92)

Copyright © 2003 by **Curnow Music Press, Inc.**

Bb BASS T.C. SOLO **3. TRINIDAD AND TOBAGO** Ann Lindsay (ASCAP)

Bb BASS T.C. SOLO

4. KUM BA YAH

Arr. **Timothy Johnson** (ASCAP)

Bb BASS T.C. SOLO

5. POLONAISE FOR POLAR BEARS

Craig Alan (ASCAP)

6. CARNIVAL

Timothy Johnson (ASCAP)

Bb BASS T.C. SOLO # 7. FAITH OF OUR FATHERS

Arr. **Mike Hannickel** (ASCAP)

Johannes Brahms
8. HUNGARIAN DANCE NO.6

Arr. **Ann Lindsay** (ASCAP)

9. TUBA HOLIDAY

Mike Hannickel (ASCAP)

10. TUBA DANCES

James Curnow (ASCAP)

Copyright © 2003 by **Curnow Music Press, Inc.**

Bb BASS T.C. SOLO

W.A. Mozart
11. ARIA
from "THE MAGIC FLUTE"

Arr. **Ann Lindsay** (ASCAP)

0850.03 Bb Bass T.C.

Edvard Grieg

12. IN THE HALL OF THE MOUNTAIN KING
From Peer Gynt Suite #1

Arr. **James Curnow** (ASCAP)

Bb BASS B.C. SOLO

1. A SUMMER WALK

Mike Hannickel (ASCAP)

Bb BASS B.C. SOLO

2. SOLILOQUY for TUBA

Craig Alan (ASCAP)

Copyright © 2003 by **Curnow Music Press, Inc.**

B♭ BASS B.C. SOLO
3. TRINIDAD AND TOBAGO
Ann Lindsay (ASCAP)

Bb BASS B.C. SOLO

4. KUM BA YAH

Arr. **Timothy Johnson** (ASCAP)

Copyright © 2003 by **Curnow Music Press, Inc.**

Bb BASS B.C. SOLO

5. POLONAISE FOR POLAR BEARS

Craig Alan (ASCAP)

6. CARNIVAL

Timothy Johnson (ASCAP)

7. FAITH OF OUR FATHERS

Arr. **Mike Hannickel** (ASCAP)

Copyright © 2003 by Curnow Music Press, Inc.

Track
16 17 Bb BASS B.C. SOLO

Johannes Brahms
8. HUNGARIAN DANCE NO.6

Arr. **Ann Lindsay** (ASCAP)

9. TUBA HOLIDAY

Mike Hannickel (ASCAP)

10. TUBA DANCES

James Curnow (ASCAP)

Bb BASS B.C. SOLO

W.A.Mozart
11. ARIA
from "THE MAGIC FLUTE"

Arr. **Ann Lindsay** (ASCAP)

Edvard Grieg

12. IN THE HALL OF THE MOUNTAIN KING

From Peer Gynt Suite #1

B♭ BASS B.C. SOLO

Arr. **James Curnow** (ASCAP)